Tewkesbury

in old picture postcards volume 2

by
C. Burd

European Library – Zaltbommel/Netherlands

GB ISBN 90 288 4957 2 / CIP

INTRODUCTION

For centuries Tewkesbury has been a centre of great interest and drama, few other towns of similar size could boast such an early history full of pageantry and colour.

Kings and Queens, Princes and Noblemen have contributed to its past glory, many of them interred in its great abbey and remembered in the names of its buildings and streets.

Wars and disputes have wrought their havoc with death and destruction visiting themselves upon this small community.

Now a centre of interest for tourists and historians, Tewkesbury has survived all the din and clamour of battle to become a quiet country town, having to contend only with the noise and fumes of the traffic passing through its ancient streets.

Pleasantly situated in the vale that stretches between the Malvern and Cotswold hills it holds a position of great natural beauty, and history has come to the assistance of nature in making Tewkesbury a delight to the tourist by its rich associations and its antiquarian and architectural interests.

Its early importance can be measured by the fact that it held one of the five copies of Magna Carta and also the Carta Foresta.

It was incorporated by a Royal Charter in 1575, from which certain privileges flowed such as the right to hold markets, the right to brew beer and to bake bread.

Subsequent Charters reinforced these rights, sometimes expanding or modifying them depending upon the Monarch and the changes which he made for granting such privileges.

After the Civil War, when the town changed hands several times, Tewkesbury entered a quieter period when the population remained fairly constant at around 4,000-5,000 people.

Industries such as silk weaving, stocking knitting, tanning, etc. came and went with perhaps only milling maintaining a tenuous thread throughout the centuries.

In the late 19th century the Town became almost a backwater when the railway, which was to run from the south to the Industrial Midlands, bypassed Tewkesbury and ran its steel road just a couple of miles eastward, with only a small branch line into and through the town.

With the advent of the war an Army Camp was established at Ashchurch with the local people welcoming the opportunity of employment which it brought.

Engineering followed soon after with a large engineering group establishing a site in the old railway grain store at Ashchurch.

Now thriving industry abounds on the sites around the town providing a diversity of employment opportunities for everyone and a measure of prosperity generally.

Tewkesbury has been fortunate in that for a considerable time just before and after the turn of the century, it had a photographer, Mr. Mallet, of considerable enterprise. He recorded hundreds of views of Tewkesbury and the surrounding district.

After him came others and together with the work of these and national organisations such as Friths and Judges, it is possible to present a view of the town which is both nostalgic and pleasing.

If anything this volume represents a tribute to those early photographers and their hard work and forsight.

This pictorial visit to Tewkesbury starts at the Abbey and follows a logical route through the three main streets.

Acknowledgements:
Are due to Gloucestershire County Records Office, Mr. Yorke, Mrs. N.G. Gittings for help with photographs, Mr. N. Preece, to Paul and Nick Burd for typing and proof reading and to Melanie and Suzanne for typing the text.

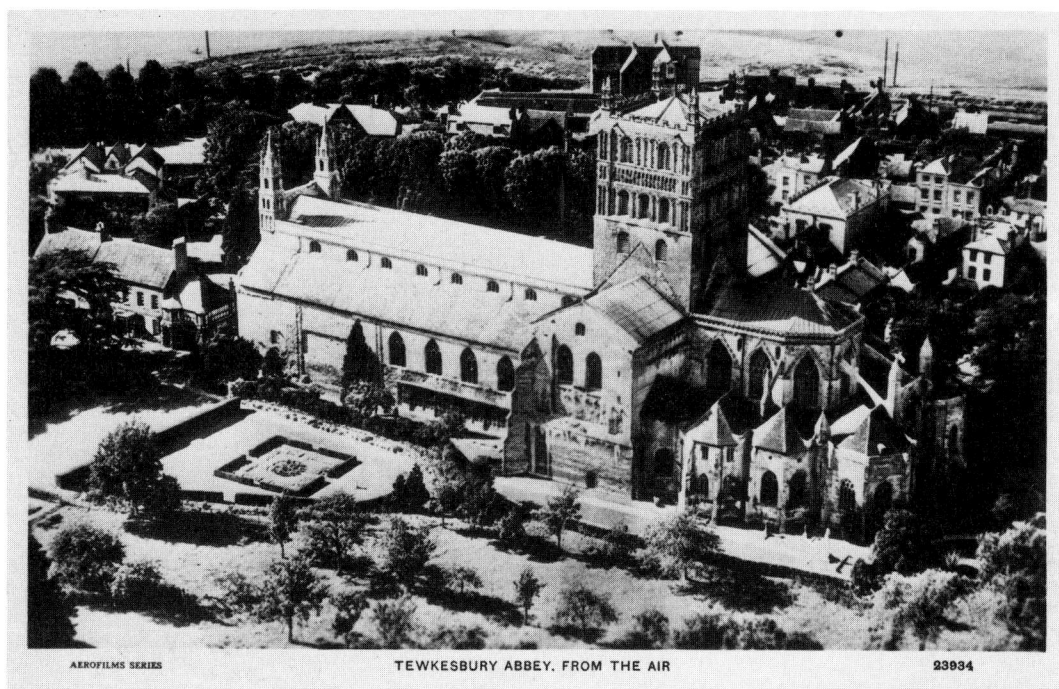

TEWKESBURY ABBEY, FROM THE AIR

1. *Abbey*. This view of the abbey and its environs was taken c. 1930 and shows clearly the cluster of small chapels around the southern and eastern ends of the main abbey building. The old orchard in the foreground has been 'grubbed up' but the view gives some indication of how the town grew around the abbey. Originally all the area from the Ham field seen in the background, to the abbey and its orchards and vineyards beyond would have been enclosed, with gates probably to the right of this picture to allow access for travellers and distinguished visitors who would expect food and lodging, especially if on the 'Kings Business'. The cloister remains are seen on the left wall of the abbey with Abbey House on the extreme left separate from the main building.

2. *Abbey*. This is the view of the abbey from the west c. 1920. The old orchard between the abbey and the Swilgate brook was grubbed out about 1960, local boys having found the orchard a temptation difficult to resist, for generations. Lanket Lane is in the foreground, this reputedly being the old track to Cheltenham, via Teddington. The lane is no longer to be seen since the development of the Perry Hill allotments into housing and a caravan park. Another of the links with past disappeared. This area is generally called the Vineyards, the name having survived from the time the monks planted their vines and grew their own grapes for wine, a practice now revived in this, and other counties to good effect.

Tewkesbury Abbey Cloisters.

3. *Cloisters.* In the course of the construction of this walkway, excavation indicated that at the northwest end a scriptorium would have been in use where the monks would have copied and illuminated their missals. Further westward was found a stone pavement thirty feet long by twelve feet wide, bearing marks of fire similar to those on other parts of the abbey fabric. Other items of carved and worked masonry were built-in into parts of the cloister walls.

4. *Cloisters*. These are the cloisters of the abbey at about 1910, which although smaller than those of Gloucester cathedral, are enriched with panelling and arcading just as fine judging by the spring of the arches at the cloister doorway. This doorway, into the south aisle, is fifteenth century and has pedestals on either side for figures. It was filled up with stonework up to 1892 when it was restored and a new doorway fitted. A canopy has also been fitted and the area now has a garden of remembrance facing it with seating for whose wishing to have a quiet moment, a use not too far removed from the original perhaps.

5. *Wakeman Cenotaph*. Abbot Wakeman was the last abbot of Tewkesbury. This richly decorated cenotaph was to be his tomb, but the abbot became in fact the first bishop of Gloucester and is buried in Forthampton Church. The figure is in a state of decay and there are a frog, a mouse, a snake and a snail devouring the remainder, the ultimate end of us all. This monument stands beside what would have been the lady chapel had it not been destroyed as one of Henry VIII's measures to swell his coffers and challenge papal authority. We should, however be grateful that all the subsequent turmoil and the later civil conflict did not altogether destroy these beautiful examples of medieval workmanship, which are preserved for future generations to admire.

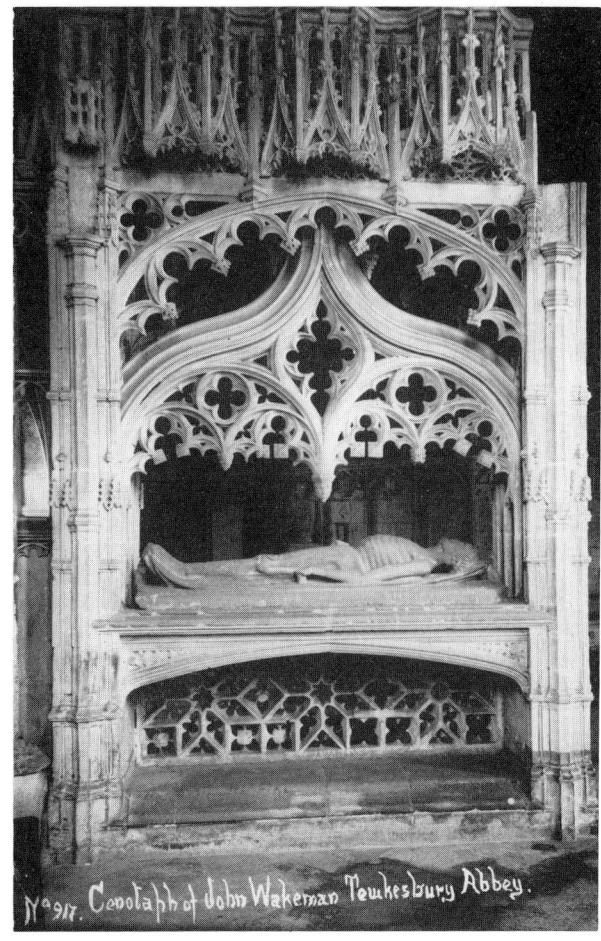

Nº917. Cenotaph of John Wakeman Tewkesbury Abbey.

6. *Tewkesbury Abbey House.* This is the house now occupied by the Vicar of Tewkesbury, c. 1920. It formed part of the original abbey buildings which were demolished by the prosecutors of Henry's policy to improve the state of his coffers. It was reputed to be the abbots lodgings or guest house. It still has some timber frame pieces of the original building, modernised and brought up to date early in the 1800s. On the left is the beautiful oriel window dating from the Tudor period. In the background stands the abbey gatehouse with its battlements. This building served a multitude of purposes not least of which was a school room. This was one part of the estate owned by the Martin family. In July 1883 it came up for sale together with the abbey cottages, the abbots gateway and other land, including the orchard to the south of the abbey. Fortunately sufficient funds were raised by public subscription to meet the sale price of £10,500 an enormous sum at that time. So the vicarage and other buildings came back to the abbey.

7. *Abbey Mill.* The Abbey Mill seen from the Ham c. 1920. Here the mill has three wheels going. There are no sluice gates yet to the left of the mill, they were erected later to exercise greater control of the river flow. The small islands in the river are now cleared to give a freer run down into the Severn at Lower Lode. The mill has been converted to a restaurant these many years and provides catering for weddings and other functions. Here in 1971, in line with Tewkesburys Festival year, the owner introduced medieval banqueting, with a Lord of the Manor, Jester and Elizabethan style music, and many other similar attractions. This type of entertainment attracted a large following from all parts of the country for many years. One cannot help but feel that those early millers would have approved.

8. *Abbey Mill.* This view is taken from the river bank in the Victoria Pleasure Gardens at about 1922. The mill is on the site of the 'two corn mills owned by the abbot' as noted in 1291. Here Hollinshed records that during the Battle of Tewkesbury in 1471 'the carnage at a mill close by the town was terrible, a great number of soldiers being drowned', fleeing from the victorious Yorkist forces. Domesday Book records that there were 'two mills at 20 shilling, belonging to the Abbey, together with a fishery and a salt house'. By 1594 there were four mills in a single range across the Avon. A fifth mill was added later but this was demolished in 1617. A local historian, James Bennett, records that in 1793 the mill was rebuilt with eight pairs of stones and four wheels, but these appeared to be out of use in mid 19th century. This now shows the areas to the rear of the mill used as a tea garden-note the seats and tables. Fine in the summer, but not too good on a rainy day.

GREAT FLOOD, TEWKESBURY 1886

9. *Floods.* This view shows Church Street in 1886 at the time of an unusually high flood in summer. Tewkesbury has become accustomed to the rivers flooding the meadows, but water of this depth in the streets is not usual. The photograph shows the street opposite the entrance to the Abbey Gateway. The wall on the right is now the entrance to the Victoria Pleasure Gardens. Reports of floods have come down over the years through the early historians Dyde and James Bennett and via the earlier newspapers. One of the earliest floods is recorded in 1484 when 'many men women and children, with great numbers of sheep and cattle were drowned'. In 1587 on the 19th July 'a great and sudden inundation of the rivers occurred. Some of the meadows were not mown by Bartholomew's tide and a great quantity of hay was spoiled and lost', and in 1673 the waters 'came into the channel of Church Street and the Bull Ring', (Crescent). Fortunately river management has improved and this kind of flooding is not usual.

10. *The Town Bandstand.* The Victoria Pleasure Gardens, which opened to commemorate Victoria's Jubilee in 1887, boasted a fine bandstand. This occasion is sufficiently important to warrant a photograph and is probably a concert by the band on the occasion of its opening in 1888. Regular concerts were given during summer weekends and evenings with this and visiting bands performing. Here the conductor stands ready to strike up the music from the steps of the bandstand. The crowd, mostly youngsters, are all anxious to get into the picture and get the photography over with so that the concert should begin. The bandstand alas has now gone although the Town Band was reformed in 1973 and still performs regularly in and around the town at formal functions, fetes and concerts.

3629. TEWKESBURY ABBEY AND AVON - JUDGES L.TD

11. *Abbey from The Ham*. This view of the Abbey of about 1920 is taken from the Ham side of the Mill Avon. The buildings seen on the opposite bank are now all gone and the area has been a car park for many years. On the right of the buildings with exposed timbers is the boatyard which was Durrant and Vickeridge, where the buildings of pleasure boats and motor launches was undertaken. The buildings in the middle distance are part of a row of Victorian terraced dwellings call Coalyard Row which were demolished just after this photograph was taken. To the left are the gardens leading to the Hop Pole Hotel. The river bank opposite is now used as permanent moorings let out by the Town Council. To the right of the picture is the cottage which adjoins the old burial ground and which was once the 'Tanners Arms', indicating the industrial background in leather tanning.

12. *Battle scene*. In the late 1920s, it was decided that a pageant should be arranged to commemorate the final battle of the Wars of the Roses in 1471. Most of the townspeople were involved and provided their own armour and costumes. The pageant organiser was a lady called Gwen Lally who enlisted the aid of all and sundry. The battle scene above is located behind the Abbey with the Swilgate brook in the foreground. The battlements are of a scenery type construction but the soldiers and horseback riders look every bit as aggressive as the original Yorkists must have seemed to the defeated Lancastrians. After the battle, which ended with Queen Margaret's son Edward being despatched, the abbey had to be re-consecrated due to the slaughter which took place therein. In 1971 there was a further celebration to mark the 500th anniversary of the battle and since then a fair takes place during the summer on the Vineyards field and pageant Meadow with mock battles in full costume and armour.

13. *T A Medal Ceremony*. This is the Tewkesbury Company of the Territorial Army outside the abbey in Church Street on 26th June 1909. They had been attending a church parade and had formed ranks afterwards outside the gates. Several of them were presented with TA efficiency medals for 12 years service, by the local Commanding Officer, Capt. W.G. Devereux. Honourable B. Bathurst was the Colonel. Here we see Sgt. J. Neil, Sgt. W. Simms, Cpl. H. Woolley and Pte. A. Jackson, with C.O., Capt. W.G. Devereux. The 'terriers' as they were known, were an active group in Tewkesbury and organised regular camps and competitions for shooting 'at the butts' for which prizes were awarded. After this ceremony the Company marched through the streets past the Town Hall before being dismissed. Some of these chaps would have been cheered off a few years later to fight in France, with very few of them returning at the end of the conflict.

14. *Abbey House School.* This photograph of 1905 shows Abbey House School situated between the Bell Hotel and what is now the Public Library. It was demolished some years ago to provide car parking for the Bell Hotel. The Headmaster Mr. J.E. Priestley resided here and took in boarders as well as day boys. They were provided with 'every home comfort and delicate boys received special care and attention', according to Mr. Priestley's advert. In 1899 Abbey House School and Tewkesbury Grammar School were combined and a new building was built in 1906 to the left of this building and provided an education for almost 50 years before moving to Southwick Park and more extensive premises. The Priestley family were well-known locally. J.E. Priestley's father had been Headmaster of Abbey House School before him. Sir Raymond Priestley, another member, was with Shackleton on his expedition to the South Pole in the early part of the century.

CORONATION FESTIVITIES AT TEWKESBURY.
BELL HOTEL ILLUMINATIONS.

15. *Bell Hotel.* The much photographed Bell Hotel is shown here in 1911 for the coronation of King George V, as can be seen from the large G.R. in lights between the windows. The hotel has a long tradition of being used for festive occasions. The Regatta Ball was held here for many years. Dances were held in the gardens to the rear. Recently the coloured glass candle jars were found, stored in a basement, which were used to illuminate the gardens in the evenings for dancing. Originally called the Angel and later the Bell and Bowling Green, the building has a date of 1697 above the front entrance. From its position it is reasonable to suppose it has a long association with the monastery. If not part of the original abbey buildings it was probably part of a hostelry for travellers and guests of the abbot. The suggestion is that the bowling green, sadly now built on, was used by the monks as a form of recreation from medieval times.

16. *Sheep droving.* A sight not seen for many years, but which would have been very familiar in the early part of the century, that is cattle and sheep droving through the streets of Tewkesbury. In this photograph dated 1910 a small flock of sheep are probably being taken to the weekly cattle markets in the town, but have been held up at the Bell Hotel. Perhaps the drovers had stopped for refreshments! The idea has certainly caught the attention of the group of youngsters, perhaps school children, from the nearby Abbey school, with the lady in the hat their teacher? Traditional smocks are still being worn by the two gentlemen in charge but there is no sign of the usual sheepdog. Perhaps he is still having his refreshments!

CORONATION PROCESSION, TEWKESBURY. 22ⁿᵈ JUNE 1911.

17. *Coronation procession*. This procession of the Mayor and Council took place on 22nd June 1922 to give thanks for the coronation of George V. The Mayor, Alderman Baker, is flanked by the mayors chaplain Vicar of the Abbey, Reverend Yerborough and the Town Clerk. The ubiquitous band precedes the procession which will take them through the streets back to the Town Hall, where refreshments were traditionally provided after the march past. The day is obviously wet but still attracted a fair number of the populace, particularly young people. Boaters were very much the current headgear and were made, in fact, in Tewkesbury for a time. The Alderman and Councillors were robed and wearing top hats, replaced these days by the ceremonial tricorn hats. The Town Clerk, however, no longer wears a wig, but the council still parades regularly in full regalia.

Entrance to Abbey Tea Gardens, Tewkesbury

18. *Barsantis Tea Gardens*. A view through a rose covered trellis to the Italian Tea Gardens about 1920, with the abbey through the trees at the rear. Statuary adorned the gardens, which were quite extensive and could accommodate a substantial number of customers in very pleasant surroundings. The time is probably late afternoon, judging by the shadows, on a pleasant summers day, with the waitress on the right providing the usual courteous service. The parrakeet on the stand is probably a family pet, out in the sun for a spell.

19. *Baptist Chapel Court.* The Baptists have a long established history in Tewkesbury with a movement which started in 1623. This chapel, situated on the left next to the end house, is shown as it was more than eighty years ago. Originally the cottage on the end would have been part of the chapel, probably being used as the Minister's accommodation. Recently the chapel has been renovated with the upper balcony inside restored to its former state. This is a typical alleyway with the far end leading onto Church Street. On the right hand wall is a birdcage probably containing a blackbird or jackdaws, whilst next to it hangs a rope, probably the only means of drying clothes at the time.

THE MAYOR'S HOUSE TEWKESBURY. (MENTIONED IN JOHN HALIFAX GENT.)

20. *The Mayor's House*. At the end of the row of medieaval cottages in Church Street stood this fine town house until about 1960. The house, shown here about 1920, was called by some the Mayor's House, from the novel 'John Halifax, Gentleman', which was centered on Tewkesbury. A roadway runs through part of this site now and serves the rear of the cottages on the right. The abbey recently developed another entrance into its grounds, with large wrought iron gates and a paved way into the abbey, to the left hand side of the building.

CHURCH ST. TEWKESBURY

21. *The Crescent.* The view of around 1905 shows the Crescent in Church Street looking from the cross. The large house on the left, which some called the Mayor's house, is now gone, as is the long wall, to make way for a large gated entrance to the Abbey. The Queen Anne building inside the wall is still intact, but other buildings have gone. The half timbered row of cottages which were almost swept away have now been lovingly restored and present an almost unique row of medieval shops and houses. The Crescent was originally called the Bull Ring and tradition has it that even hangings took place in the area. Gas lights have not yet given way to electricity here and most of the area is still cobbled. There is an obvious absence of traffic and judging from the children in this view they are certainly not expecting any.

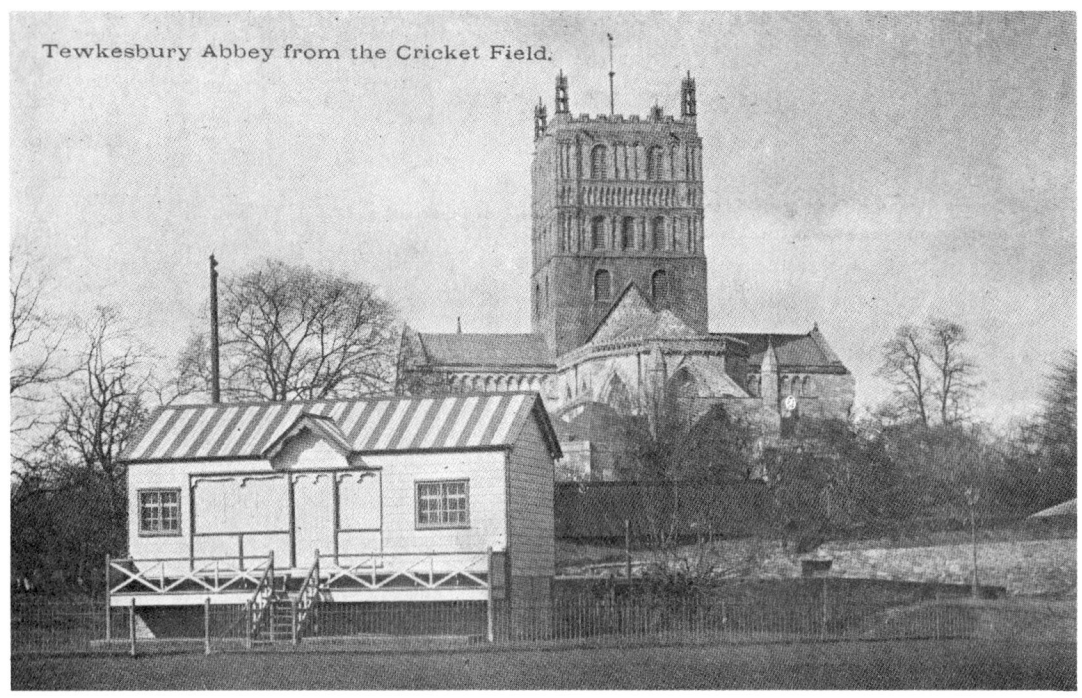

Tewkesbury Abbey from the Cricket Field.

22. *Tewkesbury Pavilion.* The photograph shows the cricket pavilion, built in 1906 on the Swilgate ground with the Abbey in the background. The pavilion was extended on the left hand side to provide a second changing room. The main structure still exists but the wooden stilts, steps and rails have been replaced with concrete pillars and steps. Plans are afoot to replace the ancient monument with a modern brick built structure so this building is due to be demolished shortly. The railings and gate manufactured locally by Walkers Engineering Co are still on the perimeter intact. The club first played on the ground in 1869, renting what was a piece of grazing land from the local farmer, and in fact has never been 'laid out' as a ground. Since then many county games have been played there and many an illustrious player has trod the turf, including W.G. Grace, & Gilbert Jessop. The club provided quite a few county players over the years from the ranks of local club cricketers, some playing for England.

The Hop Pole Hotel, Tewkesbury.

17133

23. *Hop Pole Hotel.* Here we can see the Hop Pole Hotel in about 1925 when the building was split between the Riverside Hotel, a temperance establishment, on the left with its own entrance, now closed off and walled up, and the Hop Pole proper. The main entrance was the passageway for vehicles to the stables, and later the garages, at the rear of the hotel. There are now steps up from the street level into the foyer and reception area. The pavement, as can be seen, falls to the level of the road to allow vehicular access. On the right is another building, now an integral part of the hotel, but which was variously a pub, a grocers shop and a butchers. The windows have been modified to match the hotel frontage. It is understood that Queen Mary stayed overnight at the hotel giving rise to the claim of being the Royal Hop Pole.

24. *Pickwick Papers.* This is July 1928 when the 100th Anniversary of Dickens' Pickwick Papers was celebrated. Mr. W.H. Nutt dressed as Mr. Pickwick was accompanied around the town in a horse-drawn carriage during the day. During their journey they stopped at several hostelries including the Black Bear Inn. The building behind is the Hop Pole Hotel 'where they stopped to dine', according to Dickens. The view shows the entrance into what was then the stables, garages and gardens. This has gone and the passage forms the main entrance and foyer of the hotel. For many years there was a flourishing Dickens Society in the town which met regularly and was obviously behind the organisation of this jollification. No doubt Dickens would have approved.

25. *Hop Pole entrance.* This is the old entrance from Church Street where the portico stands, which in the mid 1920's was the access to the main grounds of the hotel at the rear. The cobbled passageway still remains but the cars parked at the far end indicate that the horse and carriage no longer passes through. The gardens which are situated to the rear of the garages, lead down to the river, where there would be access to boats, and a panoramic view across the Avon to the Ham meadow and the Mythe beyond. The passage is now built into the main body of the hotel forming a pleasant reception area for guests. The Hop Pole was always considered one of the high class hotels in the town, a reputation it continues to enjoy.

HOP POLE HOTEL COURTYARD, TEWKESBURY.

HOP POLE HOTEL COURTYARD, TEWKESBURY.

26. *Hop Pole courtyard.* This view of the Hop Pole courtyard was taken from the rear of the main hotel building in 1920. The passageway is the main entrance from the High Street, which for decades had echoed to the sound of horses hooves and carriage wheels across the cobble stones. This is where Mr. Pickwick called with his friends, according to Charles Dickens, who himself must have stayed here, and probably passed through this courtyard. The Hop Pole was one of the better hotels of the town and was originally called The New Inn and at a later date The Bull Inn. The Riverside Hotel, a temperance establishment and eventually other buildings, were incoporated to become the present Hop Pole Hotel, which still maintains an excellent tradition of hospitality and service.

27. *YMCA*. Another First World War look at Tewkesbury. This is the YMCA where a room for a Soldiers Club was set aside. Refreshments are obviously available at reasonable prices and for those who wished to use them there were writing facilities and a post office service. This photograph was taken around Christmas time judging by the holly and mistletoe around the clock, and the fact that the tables have potted ferns rather than flowers. The posters and flags were typical of the fervour of those who felt that the war was a just and goodly cause and who felt that every man should do his duty. The YMCA had been lodged in Tolsey Lane until about the turn of the century. This room is in the YMCA-building in Tolsey Lane which had been developed as a club and had been the centre of a multitude of sporting activities. Later the YMCA transferred to its present location in Church Street and recently underwent sufficient renovation as to bring it into the 1980's.

Tewkesbury Cross and Abbey Tea-Gardens.

Brooke, Gloucester.

28. *The Cross and Barsanti's.* This is an unusual panoramic split view of the junction of the three main streets looking from Church Street, together with Barsanti's Abbey Tea Gardens. The lady on the bicycle is probably Mrs. Mallett, wife of the photographer who was the proprietor of the Abbey Studios in Church Street. The open fronted shop on the right is the butcher Matthews. Most of the local butchers had their own slaughter houses to the rear of the shops which were only occasionally inspected by the local Board of Health. Barsantis' Tea Gardens was a popular social gathering place. Elegant statuary, said to have been imported from Italy, decorated the gardens and the lawns were laid out with chairs and tables. The owner Palmiro Barsanti provided all kinds of confectionary and was noted for the high quality of his goods. He was obviously an enthusiastic collector of statuary, his gravestone in Tewkesbury Cemetery is also a piece of sculpture.

29. *Church Street.* An unusual view of Church Street taken about 1900 from a high vantage point in Barton Street, perhaps the upper room of one of the shops. In the distance, between the trees, can be seen the house in the crescent which has now disappeared. On the left next to the garage is the house which stood in front of the Methodist Church. This too has now disappeared. The decorative pillars, gate and railings indicate a property of some substance. The watercart has been through the main streets to give them their regular wash. In the left foreground, milk is being delivered in the time honoured way, horse and cart and large churns. The workman on the top of the Plough Hotel is probably painting the sign, perhaps waiting for the man passing the garage to help him.

30. *No. 1 Church Street.* This building, Mr. Cliffords grocery store, is at the Cross where Church Street begins. The main structure remains but the frontage is long since changed. The date is c. 1900 and Mr. Cliffords emporium had been going for some years at that time. This shop became the garage which Mr. Gyngell opened some time later and is shown elsewhere. The shop is vastly changed today, after being a supermarket for several different companys it is now a Market Hall, with several small shop units providing a variety of products under one roof. None of them sell tea at these prices however!, but the tradition of the small local trader remains.

31. *War Memorial.* Here the War Memorial is being officially handed over to the Town Mayor, by the Deputy Mayor, Alderman Baker, on the left of the picture. Standing behind Alderman Baker is the Wreath Bearer. The memorial was designed in Doulton Stone and originally had chains looped between the pillars as can be seen here. The parade included ex-servicemen, Salvation Army members and the Abbey Choir. The memorial remembers all those who gave their lives in two world wars and each Remembrance Sunday a service is held at the memorial with a march past of all the Town's organisations with the Mayor of the day taking the salute outside the Town Hall. Traffic is halted and the town is silent for a brief spell as it remembers its dead.

32. *War Memorial*. The War Memorial stands at the junction of three main streets of the town in the position which was once occupied by the High Cross. This was demolished centuries before and parts of it were used to repair the Long Bridge. On Sunday 6th May 1922, the War Memorial was unveiled and dedicated at a public ceremony. The lady laying the wreath is Mrs. Didcote who lost three sons in the First World War and to whom had been given the honour of unveiling the memorial. The Mayor and Town Council attended with their usual dignity, together with the Mace Bearers and the Vicar of Tewkesbury abbey. There has been a debate over the years about the siting of the memorial. The advent of increased traffic in the last few years has lead to the desire to relocate the memorial in a variety of places, the abbey grounds being a popular choice, but pressures have been resisted and the memorial remains at the centre of the town.

33. *Barlow*. This is the shop of G.R. Barlow at 137 High Street in 1900, opposite the Swan Hotel, with Mr. Barlow at the shop door. He provided patent medicines as well as a dispensing service, advertising pills for gout and rheumatism at 1/1½ per box. He also provided a dental service as advertised on the shop front, but this was likely to be an occasional requirement and probably where there was an emergency extraction required. One hesitates to think of the techniques, possibly without any anaesthetic, using only primitive instruments and a carbolic wash for these before the operation. This is now a store providing something entirely more sophisticated.

34. *Tolsey Lane*. This is a view of 1905 looking from Tolsey Lane to the High Street near the Cross. The building on the right is Cross House, reputedly the Old Court House of the Lords of Tewkesbury. The structure is part 15th century and the house has a fine imposing frontage looking out over the Cross. One can well imagine the Lords of the Manor and the court officials looking out over the Cross around which the market would have been held and where punishment of offenders would have taken place. The shop opposite has been a fishmonger for many years and still remains so. Here the proprietor, Mr. Barnett, advertises 'Empire Salmon' at 1/8 per pound as well as 'healthy herrings'. Business then must have been good, witness the two delivery cycles with the carrier on the front. The frontage has altered from an open slab to conform to stricter health and environmental regulations, but pheasants, rabbits and poultry still hang from Mr. Gibbard's shop today.

35. *Fair.* Tewkesbury Mop Fair in 1927. This is the Brooklyn cakewalk outside the Methodist Church at the Cross. This was a popular fairground attraction until comparatively recently, when the desire for speed and thrills has pushed the more sedate rides out of·popularity. The Mop Fair at one time took over most of the main streets but increased traffic has led to the High Street and Church Street being a clear zone since the 1950's. The large steam engines which were used to drive the main items of fairground machinery have now given way to diesel and electric motors. The charges are no longer a penny a time and rides seem to last only a fraction of the time, but perhaps that is the effect of age.

36. *Papps Shop.* Mr. Papp stands proudly in the doorway of one of his shops in the High Street in about 1910. This window shows Mr. Papps flannelette wares for sale and indicates the level of stocks such a shop would have to hold to satisfy local demands. On the opposite side of the road to this shop was a much larger Victorian style emporium run by the same family. Some of the names seen on the goods displayed here are still household names. The strange contraption suspended on the outside of the window may have been a lighting arrangement of some kind. The boater and shirt cuffs, probably celluloid, were typical attire for the well-dressed shop keeper.

37. *International Store*. Almost every town and city in the country must have had an International Store at one time or another. The sign in gold and black was instantly familiar to everyone. This shop was situated in the High Street and occupied the same site for many years. Mr. Mulcock, the manager, is seen here with his staff in 1908 when the company would have been enjoying some commercial success. The long white aprons are typical, but someone has obviously gone to the trouble of trimming the bottoms. The copper fronts to the windows would have been cleaned and polished regularly, probably by the shop boy on the left of the picture. The prices of the goods advertised will being back pre-decimalisation conversions to older generations. International Stores moved their premises to several other sites but were still a presence in the town in the late 1960's.

38. *High Street.* This is a view of the High Street taken looking towards the Cross. The date is c. 1910, judging by the shop names and the lack of traffic. Mr. H. King is the proprietor of the hardware shop at the Nodding Gables on the right, with his wares displayed outside. Next door is the office of The Old Tewkesbury Register and Gazette, a weekly newspaper which served the town and the surrounding villages for many years. Here the street appears to be cobbled and gas lighting is the order of the day. Norths, the shop on the left, was carrying on a tradition of stationer and printer in the town which had existed since the historian James Bennett had operated his business in the early 1800s. A printing business still exists to the rear of the High Street. No noisy vehicles are yet to be seen or heard and the pace of life is much more relaxed than today.

39. *Burge.* A photograph of Tewkesbury High Street in the year 1871. The centre building, Walkers, must have been between uses as a Public House. It has been known as The Wheatsheaf Inn since time immemorial, or perhaps Walker was the name of the landlord. The ground floor frontage has changed, but the rest of the building is the same. Burge's, the shop on the right, has bolts of cloth hanging in the doorway and was listed as a drapery. London House, number 131, is the property of a Mr. Chandler and he advertises a boot and shoe factory and shop. The young girl on the left of the small group is dressed in the typical Victorian style.

40. *J. Watson.* This is Mr. Watson standing at the door of his shop in the High Street, c. 1910. The shop closed in the mid 1950s, but Mr. Watson and his wife lived on the premises, and from the closure until his death some twenty years later the shop was shuttered. When the estate was being wound up the interior of the shop was found generally as it was when it closed down and must have been full of interesting discoveries. The window display shows a wide variety of items, as was the custom generally, not always in the normal range of a watchmaker and jeweller. In an attempt to keep pace with the changing requirements of the public Mr. Watson later took to piercing ears for the ladies of the town. The whole frontage has now been replaced by the more prosaic and ubiquitous estate agents establishment.

591~39 HIGH ST TEWKESBURY.

41. *High Street*. It is now 1920 and the automobile is beginning to take precedence on the roads. The advertisement on the building in the centre of the picture declares that Osbornes Garage is now providing a service both for motorists in the town and tourists passing through. This is still a quiet scene with pedestrians able to cross the streets safely without benefit of traffic lights and crossings. The constant passage of heavy goods vehicles through the town with its consequent damage to the environment, is still half a century away. Tewkesbury has suffered for many years from traffic congestion despite having a motorway intersection only a mile or so from the town centre.

High Street, Tewkesbury

42. *High Street.* The town is just experiencing its first sight of motorised vehicles in this view of the High Street, c. 1908. Horses are still the main means of transport for both goods and people. The carriage on the right, proceeding in the centre of the cobbled road carrying its passengers briskly to their destination, is a sight not seen today. Pursuing it up the street is one of the now noisy, smelly motor cars that 'would never replace the horse'! The pace of life is quite leisurely, but before many years pass the young man in the foreground will find it difficult to walk along in the roadway as nonchalantly as he is here.

43. *Co-operative Society*. The Gloucestershire Co-operative Society was originally formed in 1860 and registered under the Industries and Provident Act 1862. The premises shown above, 114 High Street, were purchased in March 1891 and the business which had been conducted in the old premises in Barton Street, moved to this site and became Branch No. 16. On this site at the rear, a set of buildings, including a stable and a bakehouse, was provided. Bread which was sold had previously been baked in Cheltenham and transported to the shop daily, was now baked on site and sold fresh daily. The stable provided was obviously for the horse pulling the delivery van which provided the usual service. Members of the Co-op were provided with a membership number and at each purchase were given a small ticket carrying the number, date and amount spent. At the end of each year a 'dividend' was announced and this percentage was paid back to members, the 'co-op divi' being a welcome supplement to the family budget. The manager here is Mr. J. Maynard, seen with his staff.

44. *Black Bear*. This view of the Black Bear Tavern is dated c. 1900. The cart is the council water cart at the standpipe on the pavement outside the Black Bear. The pipe was erected in 1873 to water the streets and for use in case of fire. The building to the left of the tavern is not recognisable today, only a modified ground floor remains as the upper section of the building was burnt down. This is now used as the clubhouse for the Town Rugby club. The buildings opposite the Black Bear are Kings John's cottages and lead to the bridge and the river Avon. The cottages have recently been renovated and the cart standing by the tree probably has its horse in the blacksmiths shop behind the cottage on the right, waiting to be shod. Prior to the purchase of a water cart the board of health contracted the Cheltenham Water Co. to water the roads at each entrance of the town for £5 per annum, in 1873. The charge would probably be somewhat higher today.

Tewkesbury ; The Black Bear Inn.

45. *The Black Bear.* This unusual view of what is reputedly the oldest inn in Gloucestershire, is taken in the early 1900s. The door on the right is to the stables, which would cost just a few pence per horse, whilst the owner did his business on market days. Pleasures were simple for the children shown here, the little girl on her own is holding a hoop whilst the two boys are holding a pet dog. The house on the extreme left, only partly visible, has made way for 'villas'. The gas lamp too has given way to the cement lamp standard. The large corner sign for 'Ye Olde Black Bear' advertises Arnold Perretts fine ales and show the bear and ragged staff of the Warwick family. The ceiling of the public bar which fronts the High Street has an unusual leather ceiling bearing astronomical shapes and signs. A favourite haunt of fishermen and farmers particularly on market days, it now caters for families, with a garden leading to the river.

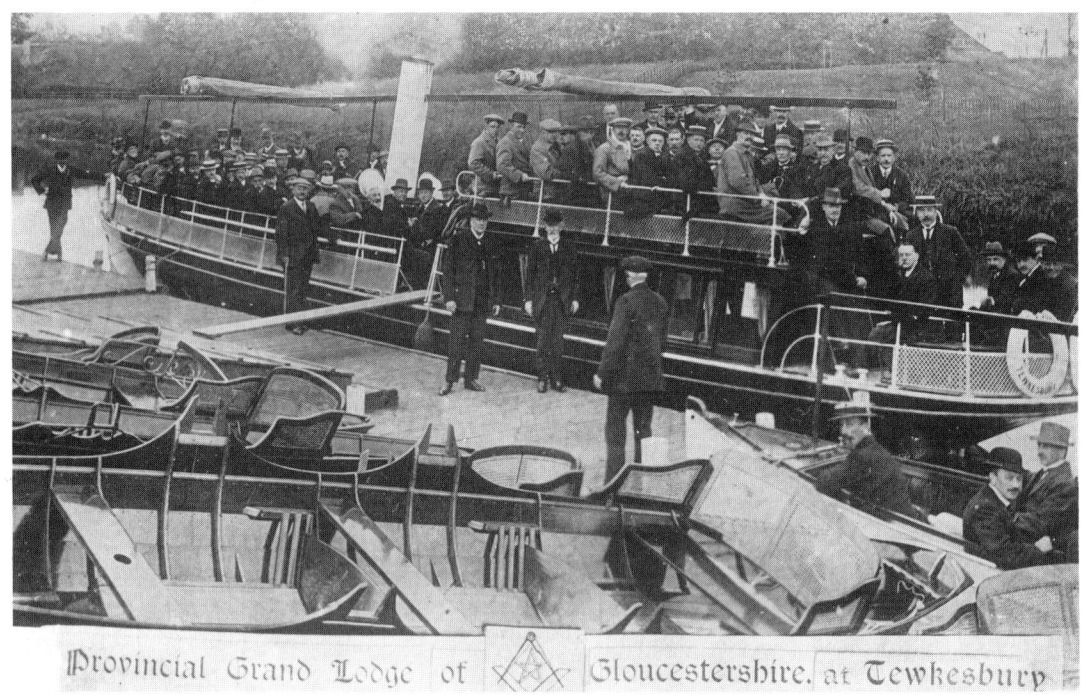

Provincial Grand Lodge of Gloucestershire at Tewkesbury

46. *Motor launch.* Here is the Provincial Lodge of the Order of Masons, about to leave for what was probably the annual trip from Bathurst's boatyard in 1909, up the river. This kind of event was used by a number of organisations; Abbey Sunday School outing, factory trips for employees, with food and musical entertainment provided up the river and occasionally aboard. This boat is the river steamer Jubilee and has the canvas cover in case of rain, which was removable in fine weather. The steamer appears to be full to capacity, perhaps the three in the small boat were being towed behind! Bathurst's continued to provide boats and launches for both river and sea work and during the war was a base for the repair of sea going motor torpedo boats and other naval vessels. This was carrying on the long tradition of boat building in Tewkesbury which has now sadly come to an end.

47. *King Johns Cottages.* In 1924 at the beginning of June, the whole of the area in and around Tewkesbury was inundated after especially heavy rains which fell for several days. King John's cottages alongside the bridge over the Avon are the subject of this photograph. The occupants have obviously been flooded before, although perhaps not in June, and have the duckboards available. The waters came up much higher than this on the following day and entered the lower part of the houses. The boats seen here would normally be sitting on what is a slipway leading down some 10 to 12 feet lower, to the normal river level. In the background is Bathurst's boatyard which would normally have 20-30 boats moored on this piece of water ready for hire during the summer months, together with a couple of large steamers for day trippers and other launches. A flood of this magnitude would of course have a substantially adverse impact on business in a small town with markets probably missed and no travellers able to get in.

48. *The Water Works.* Another view of the 1924 flood showing the water works from the Mythe end of town. Here are several horses having swum across the flooded field being rescued and brought to safety. The view across the open fields to the town gives testimony to the fortunate fact that there has not been any great development and spread of the ancient town centre. Part of these works were built on the site of a claypit used for the manufacture of bricks. In 1869 an order was made to divert the public footpath around the Mythe field, called the Brickpits, for the purpose of developing the water works. Now part of the Severn Trent organisation, the works provides water for an ever increasing domestic and industrial demand.

Paget's Lane, The Mythe, Tewkesbury.

49. *Pagetts Lane.* Pagetts Lane leading from the Worcester Road on Mythe Hill, was part of the Old Salt Road to Droitwich where the Abbey owned a salt house, as recorded in Doomsday. This view shows the lane as it was about 1900. The bridge, although picturesque, does not look too safe here and was demolished in the 1920's. The lane became popular as a Sunday afternoon walk and a town guide of the time suggests that it was a sanctuary for the flora and fauna with lists of those flowers still to be found there and the birds, including the nightingale, as having their habitat in the lane. The lady photographed is probably the wife of the photographer Mallet, who owned the 'Abbey Studios' and advertised '1000s of views'. He took his wife along on some of his photographic sojourns and she can be seen on many local views. She also acted as photographer as Mallet himself appears in some photographs of Tewkesbury and the surrounding districts.

Red Cross Hospital, Tewkesbury.

50. *Mitton Manor*. During the First World War many large buildings were taken over to provide hospitals and convalescent homes for servicemen wounded and injured during the hostilities. This photograph taken in 1916 shows some of the wounded servicemen standing outside Mitton Manor, which became a Red Cross Hospital. One has his arm in a sling. On the left in the gardens is a small marquee possibly used as a dressing station. The Red Cross are still a valuable asset, notably in times of disaster, but also at large functions, they may be seen giving their services and expertise on a voluntary basis. This house and its surrounding fields are now developed into a large private housing estate with the house being subdivided into flats.

WALTON HOUSE, TEWKESBURY.

51. *Walton House.* This is Walton House, a delightful building, set, at the time of the photograph some seventy years ago, in its own extensive grounds. It was the family home of one of the town's leading businessmen for many years. After the family left it had many uses: a home for deprived children and a centre for the disabled, among others. The view shows the front of the house with large lawned areas, a view which is substantially changed as the house now sits in a green island, surrounded by a private housing estate and a primary school. Like many areas in and around Tewkesbury, any land above flood level is likely to be developed for housing, a process which unfortunately is likely to continue with the expansion of industry and consequential housing needs in the area. Gladly however, despite all the development, houses like this continue to fill a need and are therefore safe, for the time being at least.

52. *Mr. Gyngells shop.* This is a view of Mr. Gyngells Cycle Shop in Barton Street in 1907. Mr. Gyngell moved his premises around fairly frequently and had occupied premises in Church Street next to Barsanti's Abbey Tea Gardens, perhaps the premises were cheaper to rent in Barton Street. The public who are now middle aged will remember the premises as 'Mary Attwoods Shop', which like the television programme was 'open all hours', and indeed sold almost everything that could be sold in a shop and some things that usually were not! The premises have been occupied on and off by a variety of tradesmen and retailers. Later the shop moved to the Cross.

53. *Mr. Mellor's Shop.* When the new Police Station was built in Barton Street some years ago, a number of properties were demolished. This view shows Mr. Mellor's shop in that area, an establishment which sold a wide variety of goods. The baby carriages and other wheeled carts are Victorian/Edwardian so the date is probably 1910 or thereabouts. The windows display large brass bedsteads on one side and crockery and other fancy goods on the other. The houses on this side of the street had narrow frontages with the usual Tewkesbury alleyways running through to East Street, along the back of Barton Street. The houses down the alleys would have had a communal water supply with a tap sited in the yard and shared, external toilet facilities.

THE OLD THITHE BARN TEWKESBURY.

MALLETT

54. *Old Tythe Barn.* This building is now the Town Museum and Information Centre. In this view of 1900 it is seen as two separate dwelling houses and it remained as a private house until the mid 1950's when it was purchased by a local businessman and given to the town as a basis for having a museum. The building has a hipped roof and dates from the 16th century. The doorway on the right has now been walled up and there is just one entrance. The unusual oak fencing is worthy of note. The building has recently been renovated and for some years has contained an information centre on the ground floor front. The other rooms are devoted to presenting a view of Tewkesbury as it was, and here a variety of objects are on display. There is a Battle Room on the top floor with a model layout of the Battle of Tewkesbury 1471, together with artefacts, prints etc. It is open from April to November each year and a nominal entrance charge is made.

55. *Walkers Eng.* This was the scene on a night in September 1908, when one of the largest engineering companies in the town was burned to the ground. The enterprising photographer got there when the fire was well under way. The whole building was gutted and the large chimney was demolished. Most of the adjacent buildings were saved at the time but are no longer there, having been demolished later. The site later became the Fire Brigade Headquarters and now houses the Ambulance Service. The company, Walkers Engineering, rose like the proverbial phoenix from the ashes of this disaster to start another factory on the site of the car park and swimming pool in the Oldbury Road. They were a highly respected engineering organisation who manufactured amongst other things such fairground machines as Galloping Horses and Roundabouts. Working models of some of their fairground equipment are being lovingly restored and are currently housed in the museum in Tewkesbury.

56. *Boughton's Shop*. This is Barton Street in 1905 showing Mr. Boughton's shoe shop. This was just one of many boot and shoe shops in the Town. The Cordwainers have a long history in Tewkesbury and formed their own Guild in the 15th century. This survived until fairly recently when the Guild was wound up. Prizes were given at an annual meeting of the Guild, with special sections for boots, riding boots, etc. Mr. Boughton was a member of the Town Council for some years, this was at a time when only the gentry really had the opportunity to serve as Councillors or Magistrates. These shops are typical of the 1920's with wares being hung outside every morning and taken in again at night by the shop boy with his long hooked pole.

57. *Fair*. The Tewkesbury Mop Fair has been part of the autumn scene in the streets of the town for many centuries. This is a view of Barton Street in 1910 taken from the Cross and shows 'Symonds Switchback' machine advertising rides at one penny. The fair, originally a hiring fair for servants and agricultural workers, is erected in the main streets of the town in October of each year and lasts for two days. The Showmans Guild has enjoyed a long association with the town and until recently the proceeds of the first hour of the first night were given to charities, with town councillors manning the large machines and collecting the fares. Traditionally the Mayor opens the fair by riding on the machine at the Cross and then touring the fair with his guests.

Barton Street, Tewkesbury.

58. *Barton Street.* Barton Street, which begins at the Cross and takes the traveller out of town towards Evesham. This was the turn of the century judging by the costumes of the ladies out for a walk on a hot summer day. On the left one can see the Tracy Arms one of the many pubs in the town which have disappeared over the years. This was closed in 1929. It has a gas lantern outside to light the way for customers. The street presents a vastly different picture from today's bustle with traffic clogging the streets and contaminating the atmosphere. Gyngell's shop on the right was the last of his stores, he had moved from Church Street and also had a shop further down Barton Street. This one boasted a swing arm petrol pump outside the shop to provide for the increasing motor trade, as late as the 1950's. It is now a market hall. I wonder if the signs displayed would have received planning permission today. The gas lamps of course are now gone and the Nelson Inn, another pub demolished, now, can be seen on the left where the twin gabled café ends.

FIRE AT GUBSHILL MANOR, NEAR TEWKESBURY.

A disastrous fire partly destroyed the fine old house known as Gubshill Manor, about one mile from Tewkesbury, on the Gloucester and Tewkesbury road, on Sunday morning last. Part of the house was built in 1707, and part as early as 1665. The house had recently been restored and parted into two, and the new tenant, Capt. Hughes, was moving into the northern half on the next day. It is surmised that the fires which had been lighted to air the renovated rooms caused the blaze.

"Cheltenham Chronicle" Photo. Copies 1s. 9d. each, postage 2d. extra.

59. *Gupshill Manor.* Gupshill Manor was a more extensive building than the present hotel as it now stands. This photograph taken in 1924 shows the extent of the property. The house had in fact recently been restored and divided into two dwellings. The new tenant, a Captain Hughes, had been about to move in that very day. Gupshill Manor is reputed to date from the mid 15th century and was partly rebuilt after an earlier fire in 1707. An unique feature of the hotel is that one of the buildings has timbers which are numbered in such a way that intersecting joints have the same numbers I, II, III, etc, indicating that they may have been ships timbers or built off site. There is a tradition that Queen Margaret slept here on the night before the Battle of Tewkesbury in 1471, but no real proof of this has been found. Around Gupshill there was once a small hamlet but the hotel and its outbuildings are all that are left now.

60. *Tewkesbury Railway Station.* This is a view of the railway station at Tewkesbury looking up the line to the North, the date is about 1910. This line was opened in 1885 and ran initially from the main north-south line at Ashchurch, providing an important link not only for passengers, but for industry and commerce in the town. The line was extended to Malvern eventually with a mid-station at Ripple. After the Beeching cuts many of these small station buildings were sold off and are now desirable residences, but more importantly they are retaining a link with the early railways. Unfortunately neither the Tewkesbury nor the Ashchurch Stations survived the cuts and now only an overgrown platform remains of the former.

61. *Tewskesbury Railway Station.* This is the southern aspect of Tewkesbury Station and shows the opposite platform for passengers travelling to the main line station at Aschurch. The building on the left is the waiting area used by travellers. The local train, known to some as the 'Tewkesbury Bullet', can be seen rounding the curve coming up the line from Ashchurch having just passed the signal box. On the right hand side of this line were the storage sheds for the Goods Depot, in sidings where the wagons were unloaded. From here a line ran into the town for delivery of goods. The signal box has also been demolished and now only the concrete base remains. All of the site including part of the track is now overgrown and provides a haven for wildlife.

62. *Train*. This is the goods train on the branch line from the goods depot next to the station, travelling into the town in the early 1920's. This line ran behind the line of terraced houses known as Spring Gardens, across two side roads and the main High Street and through the Borough Flour Mills to the Town Quay. Spring Gardens seen here on the right, were demolished in the 1950's and the area is now a car park where an open market is held twice each week. The building behind the engine was the Maltings, recently demolished with the site developed as a housing complex for the elderly with only part of the wall on the left now remaining. The houses must have taken a considerable amount of vibration from the passing trains, fortunately there would not have been much night traffic on this track.

63. *The Town Quay*. This is the Town Quay on the Ham side of the river in about 1890. The two river steamers are moored waiting for passengers to board, whilst behind is another boat already steamed up and about ready to depart. The boats were pleasure craft and carried passengers to Upton-on-Severn and beyond for a small fee. Regular trips were organised by local manufacturers, Sunday School groups and others for annual day trips. Some would stop for a pre-arranged lunch and organised games with visits to places of interest. Bands were also organised to provide entertainment, especially on the return trip. These would be high-days and holidays only, for the townspeople who had little to celebrate with in general. Also in the scene is a paired coxed crew practising on the river, possibly for the famed Tewkesbury Regatta, once an annual affair.

591-108 THE WEIR TEWKESBURY

64. *The River (Weir)*. Here is a sight not too often seen today fishing from a small boat anchored below the Weir on the Severn in the 1920's. Here the river is dangerous, undercurrents sweep away anyone or anything which may fall overboard. Indeed many lives have been lost here whilst swimming or fishing. Salmon has been caught in abundance here for many years, and in an early indenture of apprenticeship, it is recorded that apprentices should not be given salmon 'more than three times per week'! The river was also famous for its lampreys, a small fish, but apparently a great delicacy, which traditionally were baked in a pie as a gift for the King. Such an attraction were they that King Henry I died 'from a surfeit' of lampreys.

65. *W. Rice.* W. Rice was a corn merchant whose buildings, shown here c. 1890, were located on the Ham beyond those of the Borough Mills. The photograph, taken at the time of the flood, shows the punt used for ferrying the workmen to and from the main streets of the town, across the river and up Quay Street. W. Rice, the owner, went into liquidation later, which must have casued some distress in the town, not only in terms of employment, but for the traders who provided services and supplies to this manufacturer. The buildings were demolished together with several houses which were sited closeby, accommodating the later expansion of the Borough Mills. Maintenance buildings and a large lorry park now occupy the area shown here.

66. *Borough Mills.* This view of 1865 shows the Borough Mills under construction with the main chimney just completed, note the workman on top. The main building construction is up to the roof trusses, again the workmen are standing amongst them and scaffolding can be seen around the exterior. The buildings were modified in 1977 to bring them up to date and at that time the process was stated to be the finest in Europe, the alternative, one assumes, would have been closure. The Victorian style structure shows the usual brick stringing typical of the time and its continuing existence is evidence of the workmanship. Tewkesbury Quay is in the foreground and the mill is built over the railway track which runs from the Tewkesbury line passing through to the quay. The mill, thoroughly modernised, is still in full production and has recently been extended on the Ham side of the river. The ancient footpath, which was a right of way through the mill, has now been diverted and only access for agricultural and emergency vehicles is allowed through the mill buildings onto the Ham.

67. *Healings Mill Staff.* This gathering took place about 1890 and is a group of workmen from Healings Borough Flour Mills, certainly none of them would be around to see the mill as it is today! The view is from the Ham side looking through the building to Quay Street·with Blizard and Colmans old brewery building in the background. The railway tracks can be seen clearly running through the building. They carried goods between the railway station across the main road to the mill and the town quay. The children sat in the front row may very well be those of the Healing family, having a photograph with the workmen was probably a special treat. The size of the flour bags would give cause for alarm if lifted today.

68. *Lock keepers cottage.* This is the lock-keepers cottage on the Avon taken in about 1880. The lock-keeper himself, Mr. Jessie Gregory, stands on the left of the group at the age of 45 years. He retained the office of lock-keeper for some years and eventually lived in a houseboat on the river close by the lock. The job was not well paid but a post with accommodation in this kind of situation must have been an attraction, especially so if the alternative was one of the alleys in the town. The lock is situated 200 yards to the north of the Borough Mills and joins the Avon to the Severn. Passenger and pleasure boats move through the lock regularly whilst on holiday or moving down river from the upper reaches of the Avon. The wooden cottage seen here is gone now, replaced by a modern brick built flat.

69. *Lower Lode*. This view of 1912 shows the ferry halfway across the river with a cart on board and a small boat alongside. On the left, moored at the bank, is what looks like the 'Jubilee', a steam launch of Bathurst's. This was used to carry passengers on pleasure bent up and down the river. Here the passengers may well have disembarked to take refreshments at the hotel. This boat was normally berthed at Bathurst boatyard next to King John's Bridge. The camping and cycling enthusiasts had obviously found their ideal spot, witness the two tents and the ladies in Edwardian dress. A ferry in various forms plied its trade at Lower Lode and, indeed, further up river at Upper Lode, since medieaval times.

70. *Volunteers.* This photograph taken in 1867 shows the Tewkesbury Volunteers on parade outside Forthampton Court. The company was formed in 1859 with Captain Sargeaunt, a local landowner and Justice of the Peace, in command. These men would normally attend two or three parades in a week during which they would have worked some sixty or more hours. There would also be church parades, weekend camps and shooting practice, all of which left little or no spare time for anything else. Here the Band is also on parade and, as can be seen, younger men and boys were allowed to join as musicians. This company had a Junior Officer called Lt. Yorke, whose family owned Forthampton Court. This is probably why this photograph was taken here, after the march from Tewkesbury. Shortly after this date the Volunteers went out of business and in 1885 were replaced by a volunteer company.

71. *Tewkesbury Cricket Club.* By comparison with today's cricketers this might be called a motley crew in terms of dress, but it is in the fairly relaxed style of club cricketers. This team had played the whole of the 1908 season without losing a match, quite an achievement in any age. The match, against a Gloucestershire county side, was in fact a challenge match and was played before a capacity crowd. The team also had two county players one of whom acted as club professional, providing coaching and practice facilities for the players, most of whom would have been drawn from the professional and business people.

72. *Cricket spectators*. The cricket match played at the Tewkesbury ground against a county side in 1908 proved to be extremely popular. This wall and the road behind it runs along one side of the ground and attracted a large gallery of young spectators. The high wall and house at the rear of the crowd are no longer to be seen and the wall at the front has now been replaced with a sloping bank and willow trees. Spectators at this site would no longer be able to see the action on the field. What a thrill it must have been to watch such legendary figures as Jessop hit the ball into the pavilion, and the local side leading on the first innings.

73. *The Band.* Here we see the Town Band in an official photograph in the Victoria Pleasure Gardens in 1900. The bandmaster standing on the right of the group looks somewhat older than in the previous picture. They appear to have recruited a few more musicians since the concert in the bandstand although they still using the same uniform and probably most of the same instruments. The Town Band was occasionally augmented by the Volunteer Band and played at military parades. Today's Town Band is a little less formal, but none the less civic minded than its predecessors and still attracts a good number of younger players.

74. *Bredon Tower.* This photograph of 1907 shows a typical family outing, probably Saturday afternoon during the summer, to a favourite haunt of the local families, Bredon Tower. Built on the northern end of Bredon Hill by the owner, who wished to ensure that the hill reached the lofty status of 1000 feet in height. The tower achieves that purpose but was looked upon locally as a folly. Families still picnic on the hill and it looks as if the gentlemen in this party had just completed the climb to reach the summit. For a period during the 1930's it became the unofficial abode of a tramp/hermit, but has been derelict for some years.

Published by W. J. GARDNER, "Record" Office, Tewkesbury.

New County Council School, Chance Street, Tewkesbury, Opened April 23rd., 1906.

75. *Council School.* A building which will bring back many memories to generations of local people, the school was opened in 1909 when this view was taken. It catered for secondary education for Tewkesbury and the surrounding villages, relieving the over-crowding at the Abbey National School. It serves as a Primary School since the comprehensive system of education was introduced, when all the secondary schools, Tewkesbury Grammar School, Girls High School, Elmbury Girls and this school were amalgamated to form Tewkesbury Comprehensive School with new buildings on the outskirts of town. During the Second World War the railing here, like almost everywhere else, were removed in aid of the war effort. The buildings have been extended to the rear over the years but the school still forms an important function as part of the education system.

76. *Tewkesbury Hospital.* This is the building which replaced the old rural hospital in Oldbury Road. The house on the right, which was once used as the matron's accommodation, originally belonged to a local family. They were in business as bakers and confectioners from the turn of the century right through to the 1950's and 60's and this was the family home. The hospital as seen here about 1928 had two small wards, mens and womens, situated behind this front entrance, which catered for about 20 people in all, with operations performed every Friday by the local GPs. A new operating theatre was later provided by public subscription and since the late 1960's the whole site has been developed with new wings added, a day centre and a maternity wing all provided by public subscription. A transformation from the small cottage hospital seen here with its garden and orchard to the rear of the buildings.